Passive Income Blueprint

How To Go From Complete Beginner To 10000/Mo With Social Media Marketing, E-Commerce, Dropshipping, Shopify, Blogging, Affiliate Marketing And Self-Publishing

Written By

Raphael Leonardo

within this document is for educational and entertainment purposes only. All effort has been executed to present accurate, up to date, reliable, complete information. No warranties of any kind are declared or implied. Readers acknowledge that the author is not engaging in the rendering of legal, financial, medical or professional advice. The content within this book has been derived from various sources. Please consult a licensed professional before attempting any techniques outlined in this book.

By reading this document, the reader agrees that under no circumstances is the author responsible for any losses, direct or indirect, that are incurred as a result of the use of information contained within this document, including, but not limited to, errors, omissions, or inaccuracies.

Table Of Contents

Part - I

Part - II

7

Part - I

Click, Click, Cha-Ching!

Learn the Simplest Ways to Make Money Online in 2020

Introduction

Are you struggling to pay your mortgage, your kids' private school tuition, or your grocery bill? Does it seem like it's only possible to live the life you want working 40+ hours a week at a job you hate? Fifty years ago, that may have been true. But today, the world of finances, business, and income is rapidly changing, and it's all thanks to the internet. If you're tired of getting up every morning and fighting traffic to get to the office, you may want to think about starting an online business, and reaping the benefits of a passive income.

So what is a passive income? Simply put, passive income is a way to make money online through facilitation, not participation. It doesn't mean you don't have to do any work, but it means that you can make a lot of money by simply maintaining your website, rather than actively performing tasks or services forty hours a week. Passive income can cut your work week in half, and ensures that you continue to make money even when you're not sitting in front of your laptop (Royal, 2019).

The online business world is a complex one, and can seem daunting for those who don't feel like they have a lot of technical know-how. People are finding more creative ways to make money on the internet, both passive and active, and it's changing the way we all think about business in general. Freelancing, affiliate marketing, blogging, web hosting, and ebook publishing are just a few of the ways people are making money on the internet. They are achieving a great deal of personal freedom over their lives and their finances.

This book will take you through the basics of making a passive income online. No one strategy fits all, so this book will also walk you through several different ways to make a passive income. This book will give you tips for success, outline common mistakes people make, and give you insight into how you can make each strategy work for you.

While this book will give you an overview of some of the best ways to make money in 2020, the strategy I believe to be the best is affiliate marketing. This is a passive income strategy that is growing exponentially, and promises to offer rich rewards over the next few years to those who understand how to capitalize on it. As such, there will be an entire chapter devoted to affiliate marketing, and how to harness this digital money-making strategy to halve your work week and double your income.

The number one benefit that people gain from working online (whether passively or actively) is freedom. There are three kinds of freedom to be gained from online work: financial, time, and location. Some online work provides all-three; some only gets you one or two. But no matter what your situation, interests, or skills are, there's no need for you to feel trapped by your finances. If you want to make more money, passive income is for you. If you want to work less, passive income is for you. And if you want the freedom to work wherever you want without having to commute to an office or store every day, then passive income is for you.

What is Financial Freedom?

Financial freedom isn't merely about making more money — it's about continuing to make money even when you're not working (Hogan, 2019). In a physical job, you only get paid for the time you spend in the office. But imagine if you only had to go into your office Monday morning. You spend a few hours teaching your computer how to do your job, review the work that was done the week before, and leave by lunchtime. Now imagine that you continue to make money round the clock, 24/7, from the comfort of your own home!

No matter your current salary, passive income has the potential to double your monthly earnings. Potential, of course, is no guarantee. Passive income still requires a lot of work up-front, and its success in many cases relies on regular monitoring of progress and frequent additions of new content. But even if you're only breaking even right now, there's potential for infinite growth, and that's liberating. You don't need a promotion, a transfer, a third degree, or a professional development course to start earning more money. And if your business crashes, you lose... well, nothing. Passive income strategies require little to no money upfront, so if it doesn't work out, you won't lose your entire life savings or have to declare bankruptcy. You may need to pick up a part-time job in the real world while you get your next passive income strategy up and running, but across the board, the risks are low, and you get to keep almost 100% of your profits.

Passive income is called passive for a reason. Yes, it still requires work, but it's a lot less work for a lot more money than traditional, "active" income. This means that you have the power to determine how and when you want to spend time facilitating and growing your passive income strategy. While a growing number of people are making 100% of their money through passive income, others are using passive income strategies as supplements to the jobs they already have. For example, imagine that you are a mother of three or a full-time master's student. You don't really have the time to work full time, but your bills leave you with no other choice. Worse, you may not have the time to wait for your passive income strategy to start making you money. Not to worry! You can work a part-time job with hours that are comfortable for you, and supplement that steady income with passive income. Many people are using this half-and-half strategy for amazing results. They make far more than they ever would just working 40 hours a week at an office job. And as your passive income strategy grows, you may find yourself making enough money to comfortably quit that part-time job altogether!

Finally, financial freedom means that there is potentially money coming your way at all times. Unlike a traditional paycheck, which you have to wait a week, two weeks, or even a month for, passive income pays you in a steady stream of small payments (Mason, 2019). No matter what, you'll always have money coming your way. That security can greatly ease the stress of making financial deadlines that appear in the middle of the month or covering sudden emergency costs.

What is Time and Location Freedom?

Financial freedom isn't the only freedom to be gained through passive income. You may only break even with your passive income, making the same that you would at a 9-5. But you'll be making that money in half the time, giving you an extra 20-30 hours a week to spend living your life. In many cases, two to three hours a day is enough time to maintain and grow a passive income strategy successfully. Imagine what you could do with an extra 20 hours a week!

Time freedom doesn't just mean working less, however. It also means the ability to live by your own schedule. If you want to work eight hours every Sunday and have the next six days open, you can. If you want to wake up every morning, spend an hour on your passive income strategy, and then have the rest of the day open, you can. If you want to work early in the morning, you can. If you want to work late at night, you can.

Long story short, passive income gives you almost universal control over your schedule. Unlike "active" incomes, which have deadlines, appointments, and other scheduling restraints, a passive income has no schedule. For example, freelance writing would be an example of an active online income. While freelancing gives you a lot more freedom than an office job, freelancers still have deadlines and appointments. They must be available round-the-clock to answer communications from multiple clients.

An online business, on the other hand, is an example of passive income. You don't need to be sitting in front of your laptop for people to shop at your store. As long as the site is functioning properly, then most of your work is marketing, offering new products or services, optimizing your website, and improving your SEO. None of these things come with deadlines or appointments. You can choose how much or how little work you want to put into these activities, and you can choose when you want to do that work.

Location freedom works much the same way. The term "digital nomad" is an increasingly popular word, and it refers to people who can earn 100% of their money remotely through their laptops. That means they can live and travel wherever in the world they want. If you run an ecommerce platform, you can promote your online store while sitting on a beach in Florida, the balcony of a hotel room in Barcelona, or tucked into a cafe in Dubai. With an active income, travel is something that you need to save for, because traveling costs you money. But with a passive income, you continue to make money wherever you are in the world. Traveling, therefore, goes from being an expensive luxury to a natural part of your lifestyle (Adams, 2019).

No matter what your skills, experience, or financial situation may be, you can make passive income work for you. Continue on to discover your different options as an online entrepreneur, and learn how to liberate yourself from the 9-5 grind.

Chapter 1: Mindset

Without a doubt, passive income is the easiest way to make money in 2020. That being said, you're not going to transform your financial situation overnight. Passive income requires a lot of work upfront, which will then continue to make money long after you've launched your business online. Some strategies will start bringing in money immediately, while others will take some time to have a real impact on your finances. Either way, when you're first setting up a passive income strategy, you need to enter the online business world with patience, commitment, and positivity.

One common pitfall that many people encounter when starting an online business is what Gundi Gabrielle calls the "Slot-Machine" mentality (Gabrielle, 2018). While it's easy to be committed and hardworking in the real world, many people treat online business like a lottery or a game. "It's just a matter of luck," we think, or "It'll work or it won't — there's nothing I can do about it."

This mentality is especially easy to fall prey to if you don't spend a lot of time online. However, it can kill your chances of launching a successful online business before you've even begun. Treat your online business with the same care, attention, and seriousness that you would a real business. Setting up your website, marketing your services, and improving your SEO all take time. These things are also skills that you will learn how to improve with time and experience. Believe it or not, there are techniques for website design, social media marketing, and other strategies. Online traffic is hardly the luck of the draw.

Another problem with the slot machine mentality is that it expects passive income to solve your financial trouble overnight. So many people set up online businesses, and then after a mere three weeks to a month, decide that passive income is a scam because they haven't made any money! Passive income does have the power to transform your finances, but it's not going to happen overnight. Often, it can take about a year for you to start making enough reliable income from your online business to live off of it entirely. Just as you wouldn't expect a physical shop to make you rich overnight, you can't expect your online business to do the same. Think of your passive income strategy as a career shift. If you only dabble or think you're going to strike it rich in months, you won't have the right mentality to build a strong foundation that you need to be successful.

It's far easier to make money through passive income because passive income requires almost no start-up costs. You don't need any degrees or certifications. You don't have to prove your loyalty to a company, take out a business loan to renovate a store-front, or pay rent on an office. Since there are little to no start-up costs with most strategies, this also means that very little (if any) money needs to be reinvested back into the business. Therefore, you can keep almost 100% of your earnings, which is why they're so much more profitable than brick-and-mortar businesses.

However, don't let the ease of access fool you into thinking that passive income is something that has to skill or strategy to it. Do your research, learn different techniques, and understand how the online market works. Learn how to design an attractive and functional website, how to improve your SEO, and how best to use social media to market your website. The more work you do in the beginning, the less work you'll have to do when the money starts rolling in (Rose, 2019).

Building a Road Map

Don't succumb to the slot-machine mentality. Don't just mindlessly pull the lever and hope you win. Like any business, capitalizing on passive income opportunities requires planning, goal setting, and organization. Before you do anything, sit down with yourself and make a business plan. Figure out exactly what passive income strategy (or strategies) you think will work best for you, research the best techniques for making that strategy come to life, and set realistic goals in terms of earnings and clients.

When making a business plan, there are a few basic questions that you need to ask yourself:

1. Which passive income strategy will work best for me?

This book will outline some of the strategies projected to be the most lucrative in 2020. However, these options are just the tip of the proverbial iceberg. There are hundreds of options out there for people to make money online without having to actively sit at their laptops for 40 hours a week. Do your research and choose an option that feels right for you. One of the best things about passive income is that it's extremely low-risk. If your online business doesn't succeed, you may lose a lot of time and energy. However you've lost nothing in terms of financial security. What doesn't work just gives you more knowledge to bring to your next strategy. So nothing is stopping you from trying the option that seems like it would be the most fun, interesting, or convenient for you!

2. What kinds of products or services do I want to offer with this strategy?

This might seem like it's an obvious question, but it's not. For example, if you decide that ebook writing is the way you want to go, isn't the answer just ebooks?

Well, yes, but it's a bit more complicated than that. First, you need to decide what kinds of ebooks you want to write. Will you be writing fiction or nonfiction? Will you be writing for adults or children? Do you want to write on a variety of subjects, or just focus on a specific niche? It's not enough to just say to yourself that you want to write "ebooks." You need to know what you're going to write, and who you're going to be marketing those books to.

No matter what strategy you choose, it's important to understand what exactly your online business will be offering that other businesses don't (Fiebert, 2019). Which brings us to the third question...

3. Who is your target audience?

"Everyone" is the worst possible answer to this question. The reason for this is marketing. No marketing strategy is going to appeal to everyone because there isn't a product that's going to appeal to everyone. Trying to market your products to as wide an audience as possible sounds like a smart business strategy, but it almost always results in conflicting messages, confusing advertisements, and bizarre-looking websites.

Choosing a niche doesn't narrow down your customer base — it guarantees you one. No matter what product or service you're offering, it's almost a guarantee that there are people out there who would like to buy that product or service, but who aren't satisfied with the options currently on the market. For example, let's imagine that you build an online store-front selling handmade soaps. Before you design your website, do some research. You definitely aren't the only website out there selling soaps. Find your competitors, and read as many customer reviews as you can. What are the common complaints? What kinds of people want to buy soaps, but are consistently unable to find products that appeal to them? Design your business with those people in mind, and you will be offering something that other soap businesses don't have.

Taking Action

The most important step in any passive income strategy is getting it started. You can have the best business plan the world has ever seen, but if you don't do anything about it, you'll never make a cent. Starting a brick-and-mortar business is risky. Transferring companies, starting new careers, and even accepting promotions are all things that involve a great deal of risk. If any of these decisions backfires, you stand to lose a great deal of money, financial security, and could even be facing a great deal of debt.

Passive income doesn't work this way. If you design a beautiful online store-front that, after six months, has only generated $50, oh well. Time to revisit your strategy. You still pocketed $50, you (hopefully) haven't quit your day job yet, and the next step is up to you. If you really believe in your store, you can research marketing strategies, improve your SEO, or launch a social media contest to drive more business. If you want to try something else, it'll cost you $0 to scrap your website and start over.

You have absolutely nothing to lose from putting yourself out there and trying to make a passive income strategy work for you. There's so much money to be made, there's no reason not to try. The number one reason people fail to make money at passive income strategies is because they don't even start them in the first place. People scoff, they feel insecure about their abilities, they think that there's no way something so simple could make so much money. Often they quote the old saying, "If it were that easy, everyone would do it!"

But the emerging reality is that everyone *is* doing it. Online businesses are exploding with new products, services, entrepreneurs, and store-fronts. It's easier now than it's ever been to make money online, and it's projected to become even easier. Most people who aren't earning money online have the perception that passive income is a scam, a trend, or a biased playing field, but none of these things are true. If you have a plan in mind, take time and care when you set up your business, and are patient enough to let it grow, you can pay your bills with money earned online.

There's no doubt that passive income is the wave of the future. Any industry can be digitized in one way or another. No matter what you want to do, someone out there has at least tried to make it happen online. If it seems too good to be true, think about how much business you conduct online on a daily basis. When was the last time you bought an app, ordered something from an online store, or sat through an advertisement in order to listen to a podcast? All three of these things made someone money, and that money translated into a real service or product that enhanced your life in some way. Passive income is a way to fully participate in the new digital economy, as both a consumer and a business owner.

Chapter 2: The Top Passive Income Businesses to Start in 2020

There are a dizzying number of options out there for those looking to earn a passive income. However, some options are poised to be far more lucrative than others in 2020. This chapter will give you a quick guide to what those options are, how to start your own business, and some common mistakes to avoid if you choose to go that route.

Remember that there's no get rich quick scheme when it comes to passive income. As you weigh the options, decide which one is something that you won't mind investing a lot of time and attention to, especially in the beginning. If something sounds like it would be a headache to maintain, then it probably will be. Read through the options with no judgment, and let your imagination take over. One of these options will most likely kickstart ideas in your mind. That's the one to go out and try.

An increasing number of people are making their living by setting up multiple passive income streams. That way, the pressure isn't on one business or another to make all of the money. Since passive income is so low maintenance, it's possible to have multiple streams of passive income and still work less than the average part-timer. That being said, if you're new to passive income, try to start with one project at a time. If you successfully manage to launch one, then you can decide if you want to sit back and let your business grow, or if you want to start investing your time into another project.

Amazon FBA

Fulfillment by Amazon is an easy and lucrative way to tap into Amazon's prodigious resources to grow your online business. Signing up for the program gives you the ability to store your products in Amazon warehouses. When someone purchases a product off your ecommerce store, it's packaged and shipped to the customer by Amazon itself.

This partnership makes starting an online business incredibly easy, because you don't have to the work of storing, shipping your product. All you have to do is decide what you want to sell. Since Amazon is already partnered with thousands of manufacturers around the world, finding quality products to sell is made much easier. Better still, partnering with Amazon makes your products eligible for two-day shipping and other discounts for Amazon Prime members. Amazon also handles customer service and product returns, so your job is quite literally to entice people to buy your products.

Amazon FBA is also quite cost effective, especially in the beginning. This is a passive income source that does require some money upfront, but Amazon FBA is a pay-as-you-go service. Instead of paying a flat fee every month, you are only charged for storage space, plus a small fee for every order that Amazon fulfills for you. Since you won't need much storage space in the beginning, your monthly fee will be relatively small. As the business grows, your fees will get bigger, but it'll all be in-budget since you'll be making more money.

The catch is that you have to be an Amazon seller to sign up for FBA. This isn't necessarily a bad thing, but it does mean that your ecommerce site will have to be part of the wider Amazon marketplace, where it can be quite difficult to make your products stand out. Amazon also offers a number of little services to its sellers that supposedly make life easier, but can cause problems for inexperienced entrepreneurs. If you choose this route, make sure you do your research before spending money on any additional Amazon support. Most of your work as an Amazon seller will be done on social media, where you'll need to do a lot of marketing and promotional work to advertise your products.

Kindle Self-Publishing

The traditional publishing route is still the most lucrative and prestigious way for writers to make money for publishing their works. However, even getting a book published with a small press is extraordinarily difficult, and can take years and years of disciplined creative writing. Self-publishing an ebook through Amazon Kindle, on the other hand, is extremely easy. While you don't have access to the powers of publishing giants like Penguin or Random House, you do have access to millions of Amazon customers searching for ebooks on the Kindle marketplace.

Most people skip this option, thinking, "Absolutely not! I'm not a writer! Where will I get the time to write an entire book?" But before you turn the page, consider that most people who write and publish ebooks didn't consider themselves writers in the beginning. The ebook marketplace is very different from the world of print books. People aren't looking for gorgeous prose or expert opinions — they want something interesting, relatable, and easy to read. The average size for a Kindle book is about 30,000 words, but you can choose to make your books as big or as small as you wish. Partnering with Kindle gives you access to the Kindle template, so you don't have to worry about formatting your book. Kindle even has a fairly sophisticated cover creator, so that you can design an enticing cover to encourage people to read your books.

Amazon pays 70% royalties on sales of ebooks, which is far higher than any publisher. This means that you make more money per sale with Amazon than you will anywhere else. However, while it's true that you can publish and make money in any genre on Amazon Kindle, non-fiction books sell far better than fiction or poetry. The reason for this is the nature of the average Amazon reader. People go to Kindle for informative books on interesting topics. This is why anyone can write them. You don't have to be an amazing writer to share your knowledge on a topic you're passionate about! Fiction and poetry, on the other hand, people have much higher standards for, which makes them much harder to market through Kindle. It also means that you're competing against people who have devoted their entire lives to the art of fiction or poetry writing, and who have therefore managed to secure that impossible publication with a real publishing company. This is not to say that you can't or shouldn't publish fiction on Amazon, but if you want to make some real money, don't make fiction your only offering.

Affiliate Marketing

Without a doubt, affiliate marketing is the fastest growing online profession. It stands to be the most lucrative source of income with the least amount of work in 2020. Later in this book, there will be an entire chapter devoted to affiliate marketing, but here is a quick overview so that you can determine if this passive income strategy is right for you.

In the simplest terms, affiliate marketing is making money, not by selling your own products, but by promoting other people's products. This is typically done through an affiliate network. Every time someone makes a sale through your marketing affiliations, you earn a commission. If it sounds easy, that's because it is. What's especially great about affiliate marketing is that you can choose the products you want to promote. Unlike a traditional sales job where you have to push whatever the company tells you to, affiliate marketers can decide to promote products that they enjoy or value.

Affiliate marketing is growing as a business because it works. Many businesses are glad to partner with affiliate networks because it exponentially increases their revenue. The amount that they lose in commissions is nothing compared to the money they make in sales. As such, there are a growing number of affiliate network programs or websites that you can join if you want to be an affiliate marketer. The amount of work that you do as an affiliate, therefore, is entirely up to you.

Most affiliate marketers already have a website, blog, YouTube channel, or podcast that they can use as a platform to promote affiliate products. This is by far the easiest way to make money as an affiliate marketer, but it can be tricky if you don't already have an online presence. If you don't already have a platform, you can build one around reviewing products that you like. Many people have entire blogs or YouTube channels devoted to reviewing shoes, books, jewelry, household appliances and kitchenware, gardening tools... you name it! Choose a niche, and then find products to market that coincide with that niche.

YouTube

YouTube is like a vast, untapped mine of pure cash. The money-making potential on YouTube is mindblowing, but it's not as easy as many people claim. The traditional route is to generate revenue through advertisements. It sounds simple, right? Make videos, post them, and then earn a commission every time someone watches an advertisement. It is simple, and this does generate revenue. The problem with this method is that it doesn't generate a lot of revenue. Realistically, you're looking at $3 per 1,000 views. Not exactly a money-making machine, especially if you're starting from scratch.

However, there are other ways to use YouTube's huge network to make money. Think about it this way — YouTube is the world's largest search engine, second only to Google. Instead of advertising other people's products before your own content, why not use YouTube as an advertising platform to sell your own products? Many people build online store-fronts using free ecommerce platforms like Shopify, and then create a

YouTube channel where they post videos related to their own products. This doesn't directly generate revenue from YouTube itself, but it gives your online store a great deal of visibility, and puts content out there that's extremely easy to duplicate and share.

If you actually want to make money with videos, there are options out there for you as well. You can partner with YouTube to sell premium content to YouTube consumers, but you have to split your revenue down the middle with YouTube. A more lucrative way to do this is to upload video content on YouTube for free, but then link viewers to a platform like Yondo, where they can become purchase subscription packages and premium content. Yondo charges you a flat fee to use its platform, so in theory, you get to keep 100% of your earnings.

And, of course, you can use YouTube to great success as an affiliate marketing platform. Instead of writing a blog or trying to build a website, many people have made a great deal of money by creating YouTube channels around product reviews. This generates visibility, establishes you as a kind of authority or personality in your chosen niche, and funnels traffic into your affiliate marketing network, potentially bringing you thousands of dollars a month in commissions.

Dropshipping and Shopify

These two strategies are slightly different, but they stand to make the most money when used together. As a dropshipper, you build yourself an online website, but you partner with a third party wholesaler or manufacturer to handle the storage, packing, and shipping of your products. It's your job to advertise and promote your products, but once the customer makes a purchase, the shipper takes over. You never actually need to see or handle the products you sell, because they're all being stored in the manufacturer's warehouse. And it doesn't tie you or your business down to a physical location, because you're managing the entire thing from your laptop. So you can build and manage your website from your apartment in Boston, but your products can be shipped to customers in England directly from the manufacturer's warehouse in San Diego without you having to lift a finger.

The entire dropshipping process flows in three simple steps (Percy, 2019). Step 1 is when the customer places an order through your ecommerce website. Once they have successfully purchased their order, confirmation is then sent to the supplier, which is your third party shipper. Step 2 is when the supplier confirms the order, and deducts their own fees from the customer's purchase. The remaining overhead is what you get to keep in profits, so it's worth it to consider this step when you are pricing your products on your website. Step 3 is when the supplier ships the order to the customer. The supplier will usually give the customer some kind of notification when their order has been shipped, so this isn't a service that you have to worry about providing.

Dropshipping makes starting an online business incredibly easy. All you need is a supplier and a website, and you're good to go. You may be reading this and thinking to yourself, "I can't build an entire online storefront by myself!" However, thanks to Shopify, you can!

Shopify is easily the most popular online ecommerce platform available for internet entrepreneurs. What's different about

Shopify compared to online marketplaces like Amazon is that Shopify gives you the tools to build your own unique website. It costs between $30-$300 a month to use the software, but even the most basic of packages give you all the tools you need to build an entire online store-front from scratch, access to unlimited product offerings, and 24/7 customer support. The software is incredibly beginner friendly, so no matter how technologically challenged you are, you can craft a beautiful online store-front and begin marketing your products to customers around the world.

Chapter 3: Why Affiliate Marketing Makes the Most Sense (and Dollars)

When it comes to earning passive income online, affiliate marketing stands to make you the most money with the least effort. You will have to do some work, whether that takes the form of maintaining a website, blog, podcast, or YouTube channel, but the returns that you get from that work will be enormous.

The real magic of affiliate marketing, however, lies in its sustainability. For example, let's say you set up a blog where you write reviews of different products. At the end of each review, you include a link for customers to purchase the product on Amazon. Since you've signed up for Amazon's affiliate marketing program, every time someone makes a purchase through one of those links, you get a commission. Let's say that, at the end of the month, you check your account and see that you have $350 ready to withdraw. Great! But those links don't expire. Those same links could potentially be making money for you years after they were posted. So imagine that you devote three hours a week to writing and posting more reviews, with new links at the end. Your money making potential only increases with every new link that you post, but your paycheck isn't depended on you generating new content. If you want to take a week off, you can, and your affiliate links will continue to make you money.

Affiliate marketing as both and advertising and money-making strategy is hardly a secret. In 2019, 81% of brands and 84% of publishers make their products and services available to affiliate marketers through various affiliate network programs. That's an astonishingly high number, and one that's expected to increase in 2020. The reason for this is that affiliate marketing is really good for businesses, too. What they pay you in commission is nothing compared to what they make in sales, and it's far less than what they would pay to hire a marketing agency.

2019 also saw a 10.1% increase in affiliate marketing spending. If that trend continues, that means that 6.8 billion dollars will have been spent on affiliate marketing in the

United States alone. This is a huge industry, and the amount of money that it generates is enormous for both businesses and marketers alike. Better still, for the affiliate marketer, it generates enormous profits for very little work. While professional marketers work 40+ hours a week, affiliate marketers can work as little as three and make more money every month.

16% of all orders made online can be directly contributed to affiliate marketing. That might look like a small number, but think about how many billions of online orders are made around the world every day. The fact that 16% of those sales are directly created by affiliate marketing says volumes about its advertising power, and about the amount of money you stand to make as a marketer.

Setting Up Your Affiliate Marketing Business

Getting started as an affiliate marketer will take some time and work, but it's actually easier than you might think.

Step 1. Choose Your Niche and Method

Before you do anything, you need to decide what kinds of products you want to market, and how you're going to market them. Are you going to promote books, clothes, household appliances, websites, electronics, athletic equipment, sneakers...? The possibilities are literally endless. There are very few products or services out there that haven't partnered with an affiliate marketing network. Don't waste your time and energy promoting something that you don't love. Choose a product that you're passionate about, and that you would have fun encouraging others to buy.

Then you need to choose how you're going to market those products. If you're a writer, you might want to consider a blog, where you can write reviews of different products and embed your links directly into your blog posts. If you're more verbal, consider doing a podcast where you talk about different products and recommend them to your listeners. If you're a visual person, create a YouTube channel where you can post videos of yourself review, testing, or using the product. No matter how you choose to do it, choose a methodology that you'll enjoy and that won't feel like a huge drain on your time and energy. Most importantly, you need to choose a methodology that allows you to insert trackable links from your affiliate network easily. You won't make any money if you can't prove that the sales were generated by you!

Step 2. Find an Affiliate Marketing Network

Affiliate marketing networks are programs that provide marketers with trackable links that they can use to connect customers with their products. Every time a customer uses your link to shop, you get credit for the sale, and subsequently receive a commission on it. Not surprisingly, the most popular affiliate marketing program out there is Amazon's, but there are a number of others that will link you to thousands of products and services from online businesses all over the world. Here's a quick list of the top 10 affiliate marketing programs in 2019 to get you started:

1. Amazon Associates
2. ShareASale Affiliates
3. eBay Partners
4. Shopify Affiliate Program
5. Clickbank

6. Rakuten Marketing Affiliates
7. Leadpages Partner Program
8. StudioPress Affiliate Program
9. CJ Affiliate Publisher's Program
10. Bluehost Affiliate Program

Step 3: Get Started!

Once you've built your website and partnered with an affiliate program, it's time to get started promoting products. Be patient in the beginning, as it will take time to grow your platform. Remember, in order to get credit for sales, people have to click on your links. And in order for people to click on your links, your reviews have to start popping up in Google searches. SEO takes time to grow, so be patient, keep at it, and don't expect to make money overnight — at least, not a lot of it.

Social Media

You don't actually need to build an entirely new website in order to be an affiliate marketer. Most affiliate programs allow you to embed links wherever. That means that YouTube isn't the only social media platform you can use to launch an affiliate marketing business. Facebook, Instagram, Twitter, Snapchat, Pinterest, Tumbler, WeChat, and even LinkedIn are all potential platforms on which you can run a successful marketing business.

The trouble with using social media as an affiliate marketing platform is that social media is...well, social. People aren't necessarily looking to shop when they're scrolling through Instagram or looking at cat pictures on Facebook. If your posts look or feel too much like advertisements, it can quickly turn people away. Presentation is everything on social media, and affiliate marketing is no exception to this rule. If you feel like social media would be a good space for you to run your business, here are a few tips to help you avoid some common mistakes.

Lovely-Looking Links

Affiliate links can be very easy to spot. Amazon's, in particular, can sometimes look like advertisements or pop-ups. In the beginning, make a few test posts to see how your links actually look in the post. The cleaner and simpler the link, the more likely people are to click on it. It's also important to consider where and how you decide to post your links. Are you going to be upfront about your marketing strategy, or are you going to work your links into a pre-established platform?

Quality Content

Content is king on social media. If you're going to be a successful marketer, then your posts need to be able to stand on their own. If you removed your links entirely, would your post still be interesting or entertaining? If not, you're not going to get many bites. The challenge of marketing on social media is creating content that's interesting to viewers in and of itself, and then using that content as a vehicle through which to funnel traffic to your affiliate's products.

Use Photos

No matter what platform you're on, incorporating some kind of visual element into your posts is an important way to draw people to your platform. Even on a text-based platform like Twitter or Facebook, simply posting your reviews with your affiliate links won't attract anyone's attention. Social media is different from blogging. People aren't necessarily in the mindset to read long articles when they're scrolling. Simply being on people's feeds isn't enough to guarantee their attention. Using photos is a great way to stand out on a social media feed and incite the curiosity of your viewers.

Only Promote Products that You Like

The common advice given to affiliate marketers is to promote products from a variety of sources. While this is good wisdom in the sense that it increases your potential earnings, it can really backfire on social media. The reason for this is that social media is...yup, it's social. Unlike on a blog or website, you are directly interfacing with potential consumers on social media. If you're linking them to low-quality products, they're not just going to tell you, they're going to tell everyone else on the platform. A reputation for linking to low-quality products will effectively kill your business.

Chapter 4: How to Get Started with Affiliate Marketing

If you're starting to get some ideas for your affiliate marketing business, then you're in good company! As we learned in the last chapter, setting up your affiliate marketing business really comes down to three simple steps:

1. Choose your Niche and Method
2. Find an Affiliate Network
3. Get Started!

However, as you may imagine, reality can be a little more complex. This chapter will break down these three steps into more detail, and give you some advice on how to avoid common pitfalls as you get started.

Choose your Niche and Method

Believe it or not, this is actually the most difficult and important step. This is the plan that your entire business will be built around, and if it's not a good plan, your business will fold before it's even started.

When choosing your niche, you should ask yourself two questions: What topics am I passionate about? And is there money to be made in this niche? Choosing a topic that you're passionate about won't just make your job easier. If you love something, then you're probably fairly knowledgeable about it, too. That knowledge will increase the quality of your content, and therefore make people more likely to read your posts and click on your affiliate links. If you love make-up, for example, then you probably already follow a ton of make-up related bloggers, reviewers, and social media influencers. Therefore, you already know what kinds of posts attract attention and keep people interested.

You also want to make sure you're choosing a niche that you can actually make money from. For example, marketing books of experimental Russian-language poetry is probably not going to make you a ton of money. However, becoming a book reviewer could be incredibly lucrative! There are very few books that you can't find on Amazon, so you can choose to only market and review books that you like. You can review and link to the experimental Russian-language poets that you love, but you can review and link to other poets, writers, and books of all genres that you've read and enjoyed as well.

Find an Affiliate Network

As affiliate marketing becomes more and more profitable, more and more programs have appeared to help pair online merchants with marketers. Once you have your niche and methodology in mind, then you can start looking for an affiliate network that will best support you. Of course, you want to make sure that the marketplace you choose has plenty of merchants who sell the kinds of products that you want to support. You also want to take a look at how much commission you actually stand to make. Some networks give as low as 10%, while others give as high as 50%. Most networks pay you per sale, but some offer commissions per click. Still others will offer you commissions if customers complete certain tasks, such as making an account or signing up for a mailing list.

Get Started!

Once you've found your network and know what kind of product you want to market, you're ready to get started selling. In order to do that, of course, you need to build yourself and your business a landing page...

Building a Landing Page

A landing page is a custom web page that has been created with a very specific target audience in mind. Landing pages give customers the exact information they need to get the products or services that they want. Not all affiliate marketers need or use landing pages on their websites, but if you are promoting a particular service or products from one particular online business, then a landing page can be a great way to funnel interested customers directly to the products they are interested in.

If you've used the internet at all, you're familiar with landing pages, though you may not realize it. The first time you go to Shopify, for example, it won't direct to the Shopify home page. You'll be directed to Shopify's landing page, where there are only two buttons for you to click on — CREATE ACCOUNT or NO THANKS. Clicking NO THANKS will take you to Shopify's homepage as a guest, while CREATE ACCOUNT will help you create an account, of course.

The purpose of the landing page is to make it extremely easy for interested customers to complete the action that Shopify most wants them to complete, and that's creating an account. Those who don't want an account will simply pass the landing page by, but those who do want an account won't have to spend any time or effort searching through the site. They can do it right away, which ultimately makes them far more likely to do it.

For you, as an affiliate marketer, your landing page can do several different things. Depending on how your affiliate program and personal platform are working, your landing page can be designed to do a couple things. It can direct people to the products you're marketing through targeted links, or it can direct people to your personal blog or website. It can even add interested customers to a mailing list that you can use to send links and reviews through mass emails.

However you want to do it, the first step is to ask yourself "What is the action I most want customers to complete?" This is the action that the landing page should facilitate. Landing pages should be simple, easy to read, and easy to navigate. Those who are interested in doing X should be able to do it easily, while those who still want to think about it should have a way to bypass the landing page and enter your website.

If you're feeling overwhelmed and thinking "I have no idea how to build a landing page from scratch..." don't worry. There are plenty of landing page generators available on the internet that can help you to create professional and functional landing pages. As always, do your research, review your options, and choose the generator that you think will be best for your needs. To help you get started on your search, here are a few popular landing page generators that are used by online businesses of all kinds:

- Landingi
- Thrive
- Instapage

- Unbounce
- Leadpages

All of these tools are easy to use, come with little or no cost, and can yield gorgeous results. You have probably seen or even used landing pages built with some of these tools and never even realized it.

Chapter 5: Establishing an Affiliate Business, Step-by-Step

You've decided that an affiliate marketing business is the right source of passive income for you. You now have all the information you need to make good decisions and establish your affiliate marketing business. This chapter will now help you to streamline the process, providing you with a week-by-week plan to get your business off the ground.

Week 1: Build an Arsenal of Ideas (Guillebeau, 2017)

Before you do anything, you have to do some thinking. So for the first week, just brainstorm. What kinds of products do you want to sell? Are they high-ticket or low-ticket? What kinds of people would want to buy such a product? Is there a niche for you to make money on that product? Are you going to use social media, build your own website, or both? Do you need a landing page? Are you going to market with a blog, YouTube channel, podcast, mailing list, or none of the above? For the first week, let yourself dream, plan, and scheme until you have a good sense of what you want to do and how you want to get it done.

Week 2: Do Your Research

Once you have a good plan of what you want to want to sell and how, take to the internet. Learn about the industry that you want to be marketing in. Pay attention to how other marketers are advertising products in that industry. Who are they marketing to? What kinds of posts, landing pages, or advertisements would entice you to buy their products or services? Which wouldn't? Is there a certain demographic that your given product isn't being marketed to? Could you make money marketing to that demographic?

Do some research into your methodology, too. If you want to make a YouTube channel, find other people on YouTube doing the same thing. If you want to write a blog, find other product review blogs and get a feel for how people are making their products available to customers. And, of course, research different affiliate marketing programs. Get a sense of program expectations, how much they're going to pay you, and what they're paying you for.

Week 3: Build Your Platform

Now it's time to get yourself on the internet. If you want to market through social media, set up your affiliate account, put up a few teaser posts, and read, read, read about social media marketing. Once you know your product, medium, and target audience, then you're ready to build a website that will entice customers. If you're new to website design, not to worry. It's not as complicated as you think:

1. **Choose a Website and Domain Name**

If you're going to build a website, it's going to need a name! What's your business going to be called? This is an important step, so give it some thought. Remember that your website name is the face of your business. It's how people are going to remember you, so you want something unique, but not so unique that it's difficult to spell or pronounce. Once you've chosen your website name, you'll need to choose a domain name as well. Your domain is your digital address. It's how search engines and potential customers can find your website. So for example, TheShoeGuru might by the name of your website, and shoeguru.com might be your domain name.

2. **Purchase a Domain Name and Web Host**

Once you've chosen a domain name, you'll need to purchase it from a registrar. Have a few backup names ready just in case someone has already purchased the name you want. You'll also need to purchase a package with a web host. A web host is a company that will provide your website with the resources it needs to appear online. Basic web hosting packages can cost as little as $3 a month, so this doesn't have to be an outrageous expense, especially if the spine of your website is going to be a landing page. Better still, many web hosts include domain name registration, so you can purchase your domain name and your web host in one go!

3. **Install WordPress and Build your Site!**

Wordpress is, by far, the easiest CMS for new website owners. And it's free! Simply install WordPress onto your computer, follow the prompts from the installation wizard and your webhost, and then open it up. WordPress is an extremely intuitive and beginner-friendly program that will help you to design a professional and unique website from which to launch your business. 20% of all websites on the web are powered by WordPress, which means you have visited hundreds of WordPress sites and not even realized it!

Week 4: Launch Your Business

Now that your platform is up and running, you can create an account with an affiliate marketing program and start advertising. Before you do this, put up a few tester posts on your new website to get a feel for how it works and how it looks. Then, once you've partnered with an affiliate marketing program, you can start marketing! The most important thing about this step is to be patient, both with yourself and with your customers. You have a brand-new website, so you won't get a lot of traffic in the beginning. This, in turn, means you aren't going to make a lot of money in the beginning.

That being said, if you aren't getting any bites at all, consider changing your strategy. See what happens if you change the style of your posts, or use your social media account to promote your website. Now, while you're still relatively incognito, is the time to experiment, try weird things, and make mistakes. Once you've ironed out the process, you'll have a polished platform to present to future visitors to your site.

ClickFunnels

Before you run off to start planning your business, there's one more thing to consider. ClickFunnels is a website that's specifically designed to convert business websites into sales funnels. ClickFunnels actually has its own affiliate marketing program, and one that is quickly gaining in popularity. ClickFunnels takes a unique approach to online marketing that essentially turns your website into a sales funnel that generates more traffic, more clicks, and more purchases.

Becoming a ClickFunnels affiliate is extremely easy. Once you make an account, your dashboard will provide you will all of the links you need to start marketing products with ClickFunnels merchants. The reason this program in particular gets its own chapter is because it offers the most rewards to both marketers and merchants. You, the marketer, get 40% commission on every purchase made, and have access to back-end commissions as well. ClickFunnels also offers a number of different prizes and bonus programs that can sometimes offer some serious cash.

The reason that ClickFunnels is so beloved by business owners and marketers alike is because it optimizes the entire sales process into one streamlined sales funnel. Every step of the buying journey can be monitored by both merchants and marketers, making it extraordinarily easy to turn clicks into cash. The process of changing web traffic into sales revenue is called conversion, and it's an extremely important word for you to learn if you're trying to make money online.

So what exactly is a sales funnel? Simply put, it's a streamlined process that smoothly leads customers from one step to the next in the buying process. The buying process looks something like this:

1. Visit a webpage
2. Browse content
3. Put items in the shopping cart
4. Head to checkout
5. Make a purchase

At each step in this process, there is the potential to lose customers. A sales funnel decreases that potential as much as possible, leading customers as quickly and easily as possible from the first step to the last.

ClickFunnels makes creating sales funnels astonishingly easy for online entrepreneurs. Those who want to start businesses with ClickFunnels have access to website hosting, landing page design, A/B testing, email autoresponders, affiliate marketers, integrated payment systems, training materials, customer support, and website templates, all on the same dashboard! Not only does it make starting an online business extremely easy, but it also makes monitoring each step in the conversion process much easier.

As an affiliate marketer, you have two options with ClickFunnels. Of course, you can sign up for their affiliate program, which will give you all the links you need to start promoting products that you like on your own platform. However, you can also choose to make your own affiliate marketing website with ClickFunnels. This will help you to monitor conversions on your own site, build an effective landing page that benefits from Clickfunnels' data tracking, and ultimately become a much better marketer.

Generating Web Traffic

No matter how you choose to market, whether it's through social media, ClickFunnels, or your own website, you'll need to generate traffic in order to start making sales. Getting people to visit your website is a skill all on its own, and since this is the first step in the conversion process, it's arguably the most important.

There are all kinds of ways to drive traffic to your website, but here are a few quick and easy tricks to get your platform off the ground and making conversions:

Google My Business

Google My Business is a free listing service hosted by Google. Whenever someone searches for keywords related to your business, it will come up at the top of the results page as a business listing. The listing includes a link to your website, so it's a good way to get yourself to the top of Google searches without working on your SEO.

Improve your SEO

At the end of the day, if you want a lot of visitors to your website, you have to start thinking about SEO. Standing for Search Engine Optimization, improving SEO is the art of getting your website on the first page of a related Google search. There are a number of different tactics to improve your SEO, but the best is simply to produce high-quality content. Every post you make on a blog or a website generates keywords and clicks that make your website more visible on search engines. The more people that visit your site, the better SEO ranking your site will get. Good copy in blogs or reviews, good titles and descriptions on videos, and relevant hashtags on social media posts are all things that will improve your SEO.

Online Directories

Online directories like Yelp can also drive traffic to your website. There are many such directories out there, and some are better for certain businesses than others. Once you've discovered your marketing niche, do some research and see if you can get your marketing website on directories that cater to websites that sell products in your niche. Online directories will often post a link to your site in their listing. Getting positive reviews on these sites and consistently updating your information can go a long way toward funneling traffic to your site.

Backlinks

A backlink is a link to your website from another website. As an affiliate marketer, you are essentially peppering your website with backlinks that will direct customers to your merchants' websites. However, your affiliate backlinks are tracked, so that merchants can determine whether or not your marketing efforts actually led to a sale.

If you can get other websites to backlink to your affiliate site, you'll see a dramatic increase in traffic. If you have a social media account, you can even backlink to yourself by putting a link to your affiliate website in your bio or in related social media posts.

Conclusion

Affiliate marketing is a great way to generate passive income online, but it's not the only way. Whether you decide to sell products through Amazon FBA, publish ebooks through the Kindle marketplace, or sign up for the ClickFunnels affiliate program, you are taking steps to stop working for your money and start making your money work for you. Passive income is all about setting up a digital infrastructure that can work for you indefinitely, bringing in money long after you've stopped doing any active work to maintain your business.

In his book on making passive income through real estate, Brian Turner asks his readers four essential questions (Turner, 2015):

- Are you committed to taking action?
- Are you committed to dedicating your spare time?
- Are you committed to replacing daydreams with strategies?
- Are you committed to investing your money?

As an online entrepreneur, these four questions are valuable for you to ask as well. The most important step in making passive income online is taking action. Unlike brick-and-mortar investments, there's very little to be lost in experimenting online. Most online businesses require little to no upfront costs. If it doesn't work out, you've lost nothing financially, but you've gained wisdom that you can bring to your next project.

Perhaps the most important thing to take from this book is that passive income will require you to put in a lot of extra work in the beginning. Making money online isn't like gambling — you won't strike it rich overnight. It's more like a snowball effect. At first, your earnings will be small, but as you continue to market your business, you'll start to bring in more and more money, until you find yourself making enough money through passive income to finally quit your day job.

Financial freedom doesn't have to be a daydream. With the internet, it's easier to make this a reality than it's ever been! Yes, making money online requires a lot of time and patience, but the rewards are more than worth the time you spend getting your business off the ground. Passive income is about doing a lot of work at first so that you have to do hardly any work in the future. It's the opposite of active income, which gives you great rewards as long as you're working, but those rewards abruptly halt the moment you stop.

With your online business, you'll literally be making money while you sleep. You'll have the financial freedom to structure your life around the things that are most important to you. You'll have freedom of time, to work when it is most productive and convenient for you. You'll have freedom of location, to work wherever in the world you want to. Your moneymaker will be your laptop, liberating you from oppressive commutes, expensive mortgages, or affordable apartments that are far away from your friends, family, and interests.

Unlike active income, there are no prerequisites for passive income. You don't need any additional degrees, certifications, skills, or letters of recommendation. You may think of yourself as "technologically challenged," but that doesn't matter either! There are very sophisticated tools out there to help you create every step of your online business, from building your website to designing your landing page. Don't be afraid to make mistakes at first. Every business owner does, but online, the financial kickback from those mistakes is virtually zero. Sure, you won't make any money if your online business fails, but you won't lose any money either, and that alone makes it worth your while to try.

In his book *The 4-Hour Workweek,* Timothy Ferriss outlines the difference in thinking between the traditional workplace mindset and the contemporary workplace mindset. This book was written in 2007, but its logic still applies in today's marketplace. The traditional view of financial independence outlines three simple goals:

- To work for yourself,
- To work when you want to, and
- To retire early or young (Ferriss, 2007).

Aren't these the goals of starting an online business and reaping passive income? Not quite. Passive income isn't about working for yourself, it's about having others do the work for you. This sounds exploitative, but in the digital world, it doesn't have to be. As an affiliate marketer, most of the "work" is actually being done by the merchants who manage their online shops and the customers who buy the product. Your job is simply to connect the right merchants to the right customers. Sure, you still have to work, but you aren't running the entire operation by yourself. No matter which path to passive income you choose, this is the goal. It's collaboration taken to an extreme level, with digital technology enabling us all to do very specific jobs at peak efficiency, thereby making more money for much less effort.

It's true that passive income leads to freedom of time. You can work whenever it is convenient for you. However, the goal isn't really to work whenever you want. The goal is to prevent work for work's sake. Passive income is all about doing the minimum necessary work for the maximum results. In the business world, this is called the "minimum effective load," and it's anathema to active income. If you're getting paid by the hour, after all, then you're never going to want to cut back your workweek. And if you only need to be in the office for one hour a day to get your job done, you'll quickly find yourself without a job. But with passive income, not only is it possible to work one hour a day and keep your job, it's possible to actually grow your business in this kind of time.

Finally, and maybe most importantly, passive income and traditional retirement schemes are usually incompatible. Though you'll be making more money for less work, you won't have a 401(k), you won't have any benefits (that includes health care), and you won't necessarily be making the kind of money where you can squirrel away thousands of dollars into a retirement account. Making passive income your lifestyle means radically rethinking your plans for the future. Those who make their living through passive income aren't planning for early retirements. Instead, they distribute recovery periods and adventures throughout the course of their lives. Inactivity isn't the goal for those living on passive income. Spending your time (and money) on the people, places, and activities that are most important to you is the goal. With passive income, you don't have to wait until you're 70 to live like you're retired. You can start living the life you want within a year or two of launching your online business.

Remember that passive income won't start making you money overnight, nor does it have to be your entire income. Many people combine both active and passive sources of income to create for themselves a sustainable lifestyle that they love. Still others combine several different streams of passive income to make sure that, if one stream isn't bringing in money, they still have money coming in from other sources. How you want to use the information in this book is entirely up to you. However, it's probably not a good idea to quit your proverbial "day job" until your chosen passive income sources have started bringing in some real money. It's also worth it to keep in mind that, during the first few months of launching your online business, you're probably going to end up working more than 40 hours a week. You'll still be working your traditional job, and then putting in a lot of additional hours getting your online business off the ground. Be patient, trust yourself, and trust the process. Those few months of hard work will pay off — potentially for the rest of your life.

My hope for you is that, after reading this book, you will no longer accept a reality that doesn't serve you. If you dread Monday mornings, that means that your job is taking away from your life, and that means that it's time for a change. Gone are the days where working a crummy 9-5 is your only option. If the job you're doing now isn't facilitating the lifestyle that you want, you don't have to stay there. The internet is teeming with eager customers that are willing to buy whatever products or services you have to offer. Whether you want to be a merchant selling your own products or an affiliate marketer promoting someone else's business, the future of the world's economy is digital, not physical. The sooner you can tap into the potential earnings available online, the sooner you can regain control of your lifestyle and begin living the life you truly want to live.

References

Adams, R. (2019). 17 Passive income ideas for increasing your cash flow. Retrieved from https://www.entrepreneur.com/slideshow/299914

Ferriss, T. (2009). *The 4-hour workweek: Escape 9-5, live anywhere, and join the new rich.* New York, New York: Crown Publishers.

Fiebert, A. (2019). 31 Passive income ideas to get you off the hamster wheel. Retrieved from https://www.listenmoneymatters.com/passive-income-ideas/

Gabrielle, Gundi. *Passive income freedom: 23 Passive income blueprints to go step-by-step from complete beginner to $5,000-10,000/month in the next 6 months.* 2019. Retrieved from https://www.amazon.com/Passive-Income-Freedom-Step-Step-ebook/dp/B07MDTMDCR

Guillebeau, C. (2017). *Side hustle: From idea to income in 27 days*. New York, New York: Crown Business.

Hogan, C. (2019). What is passive income and how do I build it? Retrieved from https://www.daveramsey.com/blog/what-is-passive-income

James Royal. (2019). 10 passive income ideas to help you make money in 2019. Retrieved from https://www.bankrate.com/investing/passive-income-ideas/

Mason, A. (2019). 30 Passive income ideas you can use to build real wealth. Retrieved from https://thecollegeinvestor.com/16399/20-passive-income-ideas/

Percy, R. (2019). *Passive income ideas for 2020: A step by step guide to easy passive income ideas for 2020 and beyond*. New York, New York: Amazon Digital Services LLC - Kdp Print Us.

Rose, J. (2019). Passive income ideas: 10 strategies to earn $1,000 per month. Retrieved from https://www.forbes.com/sites/jrose/2019/

02/07/passive-income-ideas-2019/#2e650e0f14d3

Turner, B. (2015). *The book on rental property investing: How to create wealth and passive income through smart buy & hold real estate investing*. Denver, Colorado: BiggerPockets.

23 tips for building a landing page that converts in 2018 - Agile CRM Blog. (2018, August 10). Retrieved December 10, 2019, from Agile CRM Blog website: https://www.agilecrm.com/blog/building-a-landing-page-that-converts/

25 Ways to Increase Traffic to Your Website. (2014). Retrieved December 10, 2019, from Wordstream.com website: https://www.wordstream.com/blog/ws/2014/08/14/increase-traffic-to-my-website

Anderson, V. (2018, June 20). An Inside Look at the Mindset of a Successful Entrepreneur. Retrieved December 10, 2019, from Oberlo website: https://www.oberlo.com/blog/mindset-successful-entrepreneur

Ayodeji Awosika. (2019, March 21). Kindle Direct Publishing: How to Make Real Money on Amazon. Retrieved December 10, 2019, from Smart Blogger website: https://smartblogger.com/kindle-publishing/#common_questions

E-preneur: The Growth of Online Entrepreneurship Infographic. (2015). Retrieved December 10, 2019, from Lucrazon.com website: http://www.lucrazon.com/growth-of-online-entrepreneurship

Gennifer Carragher. (2018, December 12). Amazon FBA in 2019: How It Works (Benefits + Disadvantages). Retrieved December 10, 2019, from The BigCommerce Blog website: https://www.bigcommerce.com/blog/amazon-fba/#14-tactics-to-successfully-sell-on-amazon-fba

How Does Clickfunnels Affiliate Program Work? [YouTube Video]. (2019). Retrieved from https://www.youtube.com/watch?v=NBCoZb6goOk

How to Make Money on YouTube: 6 Effective Strategies. (2019, August 8). Retrieved December 10, 2019, from

Hootsuite Social Media Management website: https://blog.hootsuite.com/how-to-make-money-on-youtube/

How To Make Money With Clickfunnels: Becoming A Clickfunnels Affiliate. (2016). Retrieved December 10, 2019, from SEO Company in Barnsley | Social Media Marketing Agency in Yorkshire website: https://www.bigfootdigital.co.uk/clickfunnels-affiliate-program

https://www.facebook.com/adamenfroydot com. (2018, July 27). Affiliate Marketing in 2019: What It Is + How Beginners Can Start. Retrieved December 10, 2019, from The BigCommerce Blog website: https://www.bigcommerce.com/blog/affiliate-marketing/#how-does-affiliate-marketing-work

https://www.facebook.com/meetana. (2012, September 4). Ana Hoffman. Retrieved December 10, 2019, from TrafficGenerationCafe.com website: https://trafficgenerationcafe.com/jvzoo-affiliate-marketing/

Lilach Bullock. (2017, May 19). High ticket vs low ticket – which is more valuable to your business? Retrieved from LilachBullock website: https://www.lilachbullock.com/high-ticket-sales-low-ticket/

Pj Germain. (2019, June 18). How to Use Social Media to Drive Your Affiliate Marketing. Retrieved December 10, 2019, from Pure Residuals website: https://pureresiduals.com/how-to-use-social-media-to-drive-your-affiliate-marketing/

Qhubekani Nyathi. (2019, July 24). ClickBank: The Brutally Honest, Must-Read Guide for 2020. Retrieved December 10, 2019, from Smart Blogger website: https://smartblogger.com/clickbank/

What EXACTLY Is ClickFunnels - An Inside Look [YouTube Video]. (2018). Retrieved from https://www.youtube.com/watch?v=9T920 sOWYkE

What is an affiliate network? (2015). Retrieved December 10, 2019, from Tipalti website: https://tipalti.com/customers/affiliate-networks-tipalti/what-is-an-affiliate-network/

What Is Dropshipping | How Does Drop Shipping Work? (2016). Retrieved December 10, 2019, from Shopify website: https://www.shopify.co.za/guides/dropshipping/understanding-dropshipping

Part - II

How to Make Money on the Internet

Leave Your 9 to 5 Job and Create a Passive Income in 2020

Introduction

The world we live in today is different from the world we lived in 30 years ago for many reasons. Some of the differences are negative in that we are struggling with challenges such as climate change and overpopulation, but so many of the differences are positive. The advent of the internet has changed the world. Suddenly, information that was only accessible to a rare few became accessible to the entire world. Communication became instantaneous, and for businesses, their market was suddenly not only local but international. This also opened up a whole new arena for entrepreneurs to work within. E-commerce was born and with it the E-preneur. E-Commerce is defined as any commercial transaction that takes place electronically on the internet. This includes any website or application where a purchase of any product can be made. An E-preneur is an entrepreneur who uses the power of the internet and E-commerce to run businesses and generate revenue. E-Commerce is a $ 1.2 trillion business worldwide, and this number is set to increase by a minimum of 15 percent per year (Lucrazon, n.d.).

In *How to Make Money on the Internet,* we will teach you the skills to get your slice of the revenue pie. Also, we seek to teach you skills to build online businesses that will eventually run themselves. If that sounds too good to be true, then you have likely never encountered the concept of passive income.

Passive income is income that is generated with little to no daily effort from the recipient. Examples include things like rental properties, but for the purposes of this book, we will focus on passive income through E-commerce methods. The idea is to build as many passive income streams as possible so that the bulk of your income comes from avenues that you are not required to work on daily. Through the building of a passive income portfolio, you can achieve financial freedom. Let us be clear that this does not mean you will be retiring at 30 and never have to work a day in your life again. Passive income streams take time and work to create and build, and they do still require occasional interaction to maintain. What you are doing is creating a safety net. When the economy takes a slide or life throws a curveball at you, you will be far more likely to bounce back with little permanent financial impact on you and your family.

The key is to start as soon as you can. Don't leave building passive income until "you have time," as I can guarantee that you will never have a portion of time magically appear. If building a passive income portfolio is important enough to you, you will need to take the time to put in the work, right now. After all, the sooner you start, the sooner you will start seeing the financial rewards.

Financial freedom may sound like a dream that only the very lucky get to experience. This is not true. Financial freedom means that you can maintain your lifestyle without a regular paycheck. In other words, you are not financially bound to one company or employer to provide you with the monthly financial means to survive and thrive.

Along with financial freedom comes the freedom of location and time. When you are not bound to one specific form of active income, i.e., a permanent job, you have the freedom to use your time as you please, and as the source of your income is internet-based, you are able to work from anywhere as long as you have an internet connection.

In *How to Make Money on the Internet,* we will introduce you to the various methods that you can use to create your passive income portfolio, and we will also delve into how you can arrive at those methods. A very specific mindset is required to achieve success in passive income generation, and we will discuss what this mindset entails. We will provide you with five different passive income business ideas to use in 2020 and go in-depth into the method we recommend most highly—affiliate marketing.

If the idea of being financially free and being able to choose where and when you work sounds good to you, then read on, as your future awaits you.

Chapter 1: The E-Preneur Mindset

A large part of success in E-commerce and the building of a passive income portfolio is your mindset. Thankfully, that is something that you can control.

As with any business, building an E-business take self-discipline and commitment. You need to completely commit yourself to the journey so that when you reach the inevitable, occasional obstacle, you are mentally strong enough to overcome them.

Building any business never happens overnight, and the same is true for online businesses. A great image to use to imagine what building a business is like is the Success Iceberg. When you look at an iceberg, no matter how big it may be, the part that you see above the water is actually a very small portion of the iceberg as a whole. The biggest portion of the iceberg is underwater, and you can't see it. Business is the same. The portion of a business that you see in the world, no matter how large, is only the end-product.

The part that you don't see is all the hard work, tears, frustration, and persistence that it took to create that business. As you enter your online business journey, this is something that you need to understand and accept. If hard work scares you, then you are likely better off continuing to work for a boss. This is not to say that you cannot work smart and in this way reduce the hard work.

Planning is also a very important part of your mindset. It may be tempting to just jump into an idea without researching it thoroughly as the excitement takes hold of you. Unfortunately, businesses that are not properly researched and planned are doomed to fail. Luckily, we've done a lot of the research for you in *How to Make Money on the Internet* and other titles in our range, so by purchasing this book, you've already made a huge leap in the right direction.

Once you have committed yourself to the hard work involved and properly researched and planned your idea, the next most important part of your online business building journey is visualizing your dream. Words are important, but pictures and feelings impact the mind far more significantly. As part of your mental preparation for your journey, you will want to visualize what it is going to be like to have your passive income portfolio up and running. You have to close your eyes to do this to avoid any distractions and then picture in your mind what your idea of success will be like. Don't just picture generalities, picture details. What will you feel like—other than just happy? What will you be doing? How will you be doing it? How will your loved ones be impacted? What value will you be adding to the world? This visualization is going to be your constant sounding board. Any time you feel like giving up, remember what that success felt and looked like. If you are generally not very good at self-motivating, this step is going to be key for you because if you do it well, it will, without fail, re-motivate you at every step.

Positivity is not a nice-to-have when you are building an E-business; it is a necessity. If you allow negativity to start dragging you down, you will give up, and sadly, you will never know how close you were to success because quitting is permanent. Imagine a treasure hunter digging a tunnel that he believes leads to a chest of gold. The digging is tiring, and the ground is hard. The treasure hunter becomes exhausted, and eventually, after days of digging, he convinces himself that he's wasting his time and walks away from the tunnel he's already dug. Later that same day, another treasure hunter comes along and continues digging that same tunnel. After removing just two shovels of dirt, he hits the treasure chest and he's a millionaire. When the first treasure hunter gave up, he had no idea how close he was to success. Every time you feel like giving up, think about the fact that you could be just two shovels of dirt away from your goal.

You will never be able to plan for every eventuality, but it is important to have a general idea of where you are going and how you are going to get there. You can do this by developing a business roadmap. Just like roadmaps that we use to get us from one point to another, a business roadmap is intended to get you from your existing point to your ideal end-point. You can plot out very general stages for your business roadmap that could include:

- Acquiring resources
- Building your website
- Monetizing your website
- Acquiring your revenue

- Delivering value to your customers

By building this roadmap, you give yourself an overview of what to expect so that you can mentally prepare yourself for each stage, and you can know in advance if you may need to call in help for anything.

Asking for help is something all successful entrepreneurs do. Successful entrepreneurs understand their strengths and their weaknesses, and they are willing to allow others to handle the parts of their business-building processes that they know are better outsourced. A successful entrepreneur does not pretend to be an expert in all things, and although you need to be willing to ask for help, that does not mean that you lose ownership of the success of what others are doing for you. Ask for help, but always remember that the ultimate responsibility lies with you.

It can be easy to get lost in the planning and preparation stages and simply never get going. An action mindset is vitally important to an entrepreneur.

Do not allow yourself to be fooled; there is a major shift in mindset required in the transition from being an employee to being an entrepreneur, and some are not capable of making that shift. Understanding your own motivation is important. Why do you want to do this? If your answer is "to make money," that's not good enough. Why do you want to make money? What do you want to do with it? Is it really money you want or something that money can buy you, like freedom or more time with your family? Once you fully and deeply understand your motivation, you can continually refer to that so you can keep yourself going in difficult times.

Be prepared to make slow progress and celebrate the small wins. You will soon become unmotivated if you plan only to be happy when you're making money from your business. Celebrate every accomplishment along the way as every step is moving you toward your goal.

Allow yourself to make mistakes. You will never learn anything if you don't do anything incorrectly the first time. Mistakes are merely stepping stones to success. In the same vein, it is vital to remain teachable and learn continuously. Get yourself into the habit of learning and applying that knowledge and then learn something else and apply that too. In this way, you won't consume reams of material and forget everything the minute you start your business.

Keep in mind that the whole point of what you are doing is so you can enjoy your life. By the same token, you should enjoy your business. Do your best to choose an area of E-commerce that you are passionate about and excites you. If you do what you love, you will never work a day in your life.

To maintain this mindset, you need to ensure that you surround yourself with like-minded people. Join E-commerce groups on social media or attend networking breakfasts. Speak to other people who are on the same journey. Not only will you no longer feel so alone, but you will undoubtedly get fresh ideas and find solutions to some of your problems. Having a mentor, if possible, is great as well. Try to find someone you can look up to, and even if you are only following them on social media or YouTube and not having personal contact with them, you will always have something to aspire to. It also helps to know that even the most successful people started somewhere.

Don't allow yourself to get so caught up in the process that you don't pause for a minute to look back at how far you've come. Be proud of yourself, accept congratulations from others, and enjoy your success. Then allow that moment to fire you up to continue going further and achieving more (Anderson, 2018).

Chapter 2: The Top 5 Passive Income Businesses to Start in 2020

Now that you have put yourself into the right mindset to be a successful E-preneur, you can consider the options that you have to make passive income. Options for passive income are developing daily. In this chapter, we will present five of the most popular and well-established methods of earning passive income. We will explain the pros and cons of each method and give you an indication of how long it could take for you to start earning money from each method.

Amazon FBA

What Is It?

The letters "FBA" in the name of this method stand for Fulfilment by Amazon. The idea behind this method is that you have a product to sell and Amazon stocks and sells it for you and then pays you the proceeds to you.

How Does It Work?

If you have a physical product you wish to sell, you will send the items to Amazon. They will stock it in one of their warehouses, and when a customer orders one of the items, Amazon will pick, pack, and ship it on your behalf. They will also handle any returns and refunds.

What Resources Do You Need?

You only need the physical product that you want to sell. These can be new items that your business makes, or it can be second-hand items. It depends on the business you are in. You will need to be able to log in to Amazon's website regularly to ensure that your inventory is kept up-to-date. Depending on how highly your products rank on the website, you may or may not need to do additional advertising and marketing. You must also be aware that you are responsible for sales tax. When your product is being purchased out of different warehouses across different states, it can be challenging to calculate exactly how much sales tax you should be paying.

Advantages

The advantage of using Amazon FBA to sell your products is that you are placing your them on an E-commerce marketplace that has a substantial customer base. Also, you don't need to invest in an E-commerce store or website as you will be using Amazon's site. You save time and money because you won't need to handle the processing and shipping of orders. Amazon is one of the most advanced E-commerce fulfillment services in the world, and it is known for excellent customer service.

Disadvantages

One of the disadvantages, of course, is that this service is not free. Amazon charges you storage and fulfillment fees, so even if you are not selling, you still have the storage expense. Also,you don't get paid for your sale immediately. Amazon pays its sellers every two weeks. With Amazon handling your returns (and their returns process being so easy), you may see more returns of your product. Amazon has strict guidelines on how to prepare your product before it is shipped to the buyer, and it can take some getting used to (Carragher, n.d.).

How Long Before I Make Money?

This is a difficult question to answer as it really depends on how long it takes for you to get your first sale. If you get your first sale the minute your products go live Amazon's website, then you'll earn money within two weeks, but it can take a few weeks or even months for your products to gain traction.

Kindle Direct Publishing

What Is It?

Kindle Direct Publishing (KDP) is a self-publishing service for digital books through Amazon. It allows you to self-publish your book without any outside assistance and sell it on the Amazon website.

How Does It Work?

The logical first step is to have a book written in e-Book format and formatted to Amazon's requirements. The next step is to create a Kindle Direct Publishing account. You will then follow all of the information required by the KDP system, which includes your book's title, information about the book, and a book description. You will be required to select seven keywords that buyers can use to search for books that fit a topic or genre. You will be required to select two categories into which your book falls. You are then required to upload your book cover and the file containing your manuscript. The final step is to set your pricing, then click 'publish,' and you are done.

What Resources Do You Need?

A book written and formatted to KDP specifications (which can be found on their website) is the primary resource. It is imperative to ensure that you are putting out a quality product, so even if you are a proficient writer, it is important to have a qualified editor edit your book before publishing. You will also need a well-designed digital book cover (also formatted to KDP specifications). You will need to do a significant amount of advertising and marketing of your own in the beginning so that the world can be made aware of your fantastic new book. Once you have an existing following, this becomes easier, but your first book will undoubtedly take a significant amount of marketing to get the sales rolling.

Advantages

The main advantage of using KDP is that you can publish your book without going through a publishing house or other type of self-publishing business. The KDP process is free, and you will receive a higher percentage of your book-sale profit than you would if you published traditionally. Of course, having your book on the Amazon website is a huge benefit in and of itself as they have an amazing reach.

Disadvantages

The reading public is well-aware that books sold through KDP have not been through a traditional publishing process, which includes vetting of the manuscript and editing, so they rely heavily on the reviews to judge the quality of a book before they buy it. It is up to you to encourage as many people as possible to review your book and give it a high rating. This form of publishing requires a huge amount of initial work from the author in terms of advertising and marketing. To generate sales and reviews, you will most likely need to offer the book at a very low price for an initial period.

How Long Before I Make Money?

KDP pays authors 60 days after the month the royalties are earned. If you sell a book in August, you will be paid your portion for that sale in October. There is, however, a minimum threshold that you need to earn before KDP will pay you (Awosika, 2019).

Affiliate Marketing

What Is It?

Generally speaking, affiliate marketing is an agreement made between an online retailer and an external website owner to pay commission for traffic or sales directed to the online retailer from the external website. Many different online retailers offer affiliate agreements, including Amazon. Affiliate marketing is the easiest and most popular method of earning passive income.

Essentially, you are promoting another company's product and earning a commission if a customer purchases through a referral from you.

How Does It Work?

Once your website, blog, YouTube channel or podcast is set up, you will apply to online retailers to be included in their affiliate program. How you advertise your affiliate's products and how your sales will be tracked depends on the nature of your platform. If you have a website or blog, your affiliate partner will most likely provide you with specialized links to embed on your site when you advertise their product. When a visitor to your website or blog clicks on that link, it will take them to the affiliate's website. If they purchase the item, your referral links will be tracked with that transaction, and your affiliate partner will be notified that you are owed a commission. If you run a YouTube channel or podcast, your affiliate will usually give you a code word to use in the sales cart or special section on their website to send your viewers/listeners to in order to purchase the product and have it registered as a referral sale. You will then be paid an agreed commission on the sales you have generated.

What Resources Do You Need?

You will only need the platform—website, blog, YouTube channel, or podcast—that you plan to use to host the affiliate links.

Advantages

Affiliate marketing is the truest form of passive income because once you have created the content, you leave the rest up to the consumers of your content. This method is extremely versatile and lends itself to any niche. The advantage for the merchant is that they are not paying for advertising unless they sell something. It is, therefore, relatively easy to convince merchants who are currently not using affiliate marketing to allow you to market their product in this way.

Disadvantages

The only disadvantages to affiliate marketing would be merchant-specific; for instance, with the Amazon affiliate program, you must sell three items within the first 180 days to remain in the program. Some merchants are quite specific about how much traffic your site must be getting to qualify for their affiliate program.

How Long Before I Make Money?

Generally, this will depend on the merchant as some will usually put a 60-day hold on paying out to facilitate any returns, and others will have a minimum threshold of commission that needs to be met to pay the marketer.

YouTube

What Is It?

YouTube is the largest video-sharing platform in the world. It has over 90 million users, and about 500 hours of video are uploaded to it every minute. Within this platform, you would create a channel to upload videos related to your content or niche. There are several ways to make passive income using YouTube.

How Does It Work?

The most common way to earn money from YouTube is through their advertisements. If you've ever watched a video on YouTube, you would have likely noticed that there are ads in the videos. The YouTube channel gets paid a fee for allowing those ads to appear in their videos. For any of the monetization features on YouTube, your channel must have at least 1000 subscribers and 4000 watch hours. You must also open a Google Adsense account. From there, you can become a YouTube Partner and take advantage of any of their monetization forms including ads, YouTube premium member commissions, channel memberships, and their merchandise shelf.

What Resources Do You Need?

You will need the resources required to record, edit, and upload high-quality videos to YouTube.

Advantages

After creating the original content, you don't really need to do anything else and you will generate passive income from many of the monetizations methods without doing any more work. If your YouTube channel works in tandem with your brand, then you are generating brand awareness and passive income in one go.

Disadvantages

YouTube is very strict about the type of content it will monetize. Anything that is seen as controversial could be demonetized. It takes some time to build up your subscribers and watch hours to YouTube's required level (Cooper, 2019).

How Long Before I Make Money?

This all depends on how long it takes you to get to YouTube's required number of subscribers and watch hours. Some channels manage it in weeks, and others take years. It will really depend on how much effort you put in to getting subscribers and encouraging them to watch your videos.

Dropshipping/Shopify

What Is It?

Dropshipping is a form of E-tail where the seller does not keep stock of the products themselves, but when they receive an order, they buy it online from a third-party and it is sent from that third-party to the customer. Shopify is an example of a dropship facilitation website.

How Does It Work?

The Shopify website provides you with a facility to open your online store. This store can be linked to your website, or it can stand alone on the Shopify website. Shopify has built-in services that help you to find product suppliers in your area or country. Once you have set up your E-store and arranged your suppliers, you can start advertising. As soon as you make your first sale, Shopify will facilitate the payment and make sure that both you and the supplier get paid.

What Resources Do You Need?

You would only need access to a computer and the internet to get started.

Advantages

By using dropshipping, you can test the market popularity of various products without actually having to stock them.

Dropshipping saves the cost of buying products and warehousing them.

Disadvantages

Dealing with multiple suppliers can be tricky as their mistakes are your mistakes. When customers choose to purchase products from multiple different suppliers, the shipping costs can add up and you cannot pass that on to the customer if they have placed one order for all the items. You also make very low margins with dropshipping as there are many partners involved who need to get paid. Keeping track of inventory with dropshipping suppliers can be challenging.

How Long Before I Make Money?

This all depends on how long it takes to get your first customer, which in turn depends on how much you put into advertising and marketing (What is Dropshipping, n.d.).

Chapter 3: Why Affiliate Marketing Makes the Most Sense (and Dollars)

Now that we have looked at various methods we can use to generate passive income, we will focus on the method that is easiest to implement, the quickest to generate revenue, and has the biggest growth of all methods: affiliate marketing.

Eighty-one percent of brands in the United States use affiliate marketing to expand the reach of their products. This number is increasing by 10.1 percent each year, which means that by 2020, the affiliate marketing industry will be worth $6.8 billion.

As we explained in chapter 2, affiliate marketing is the process whereby an affiliate will promote a product in return for a set commission when a sale is generated from that promotion. The key to affiliate marketing is that the process leverages the strengths of various parties involved to spread the responsibility of sales generation.

The three parties involved in affiliate marketing are:

- The merchant or seller, i.e., the party with the product for sale.
- The affiliate or promoter, i.e., the party with the platform where the product will be promoted.
- The customer, i.e., the party who will visit the platform of the affiliate and proceed to the merchant to purchase the product.

The merchant or seller can be a solo entrepreneur or a large company, and their product can be a physical item or a service. The affiliate or promotor can also take many forms, with the only requirement being that they have a platform to reach an audience to promote the product. Such platforms can include a website, blog, YouTube channel, or podcast. Social media influencers can also be affiliates. The consumer is the driving force behind affiliate marketing. Their purchases are the goal of both the merchant and the affiliate (Enfroy, 2019).

The access to a niche, targeted audience is the most significant difference between traditional advertising and affiliate marketing. When businesses use traditional marketing methods to promote their products, it is often a hit-or-miss affair. You may reach your audience, or you may not. With affiliate marketing, the merchant is choosing affiliates who have platforms that are already interacting with their target niche. The merchant is guaranteed to reach their target customers. Affiliate marketing works best if the affiliate is truly sold on the product they are promoting. Consumers can sense commitment and passion, and when an affiliate is excited about a product or service, it creates a sense of urgency to share in that excitement. In affiliate marketing, the merchant is also leveraging off relationships and reputations. If the affiliate has created the platform correctly, they should have an audience who values their input and that relationship becomes the selling point.

Therefore, as a future affiliate, your most important task in setting yourself up for future success in affiliate marketing is to create a platform that already provides value so that when you promote merchants, your audience will automatically see this as an additional value.

Up until this point, we have referenced a sale as the ultimate goal for the affiliate marketer to get paid, but this is not always the case. Depending on the merchant and the length of their sales cycle, they may be willing to pay you commission for helping them to reach other points in the sales funnel.

Some merchants will pay for leads. The nature of lead completion will differ. It could be that the merchant requires the customer to complete an application form or subscribe to a newsletter. If the customer clicks through your affiliate link to complete this action or uses a referral code issued to you, you will be paid an agreed amount for this lead.

Another method is pay per click or PPC. In this method of affiliate marketing, you will get paid if a customer clicks on an ad or link that takes them to the merchant's site. The most common example of PPC affiliate marketing is Google Adsense.

Affiliate marketing has several benefits, which include:

- The generation of passive income. Once you have established your platform and set up your content, there is very little else you need to do.

- No involvement in customer support. Dealing with the customer is the merchant's responsibility.
- Location freedom. You can run your affiliate marketing endeavors from anywhere in the world as long as you have an internet connection.
- Affiliate marketing is cost-effective for everyone. The merchant only pays you if you achieve the goal that has been set out in the agreement. The affiliate has very little capital outlay to get their affiliate marketing business going. The customer doesn't pay any more for the product through an affiliate link than they would if they went directly to the merchant themselves.

Different Platforms to Use for Affiliate Marketing

Blogs

Blogs are one of the most popular platforms for affiliate marketing. The reason for this is that the very nature of blogs means that there is a niche market reading the blog, and the blogger has a relationship with those readers. Depending on the topic, a good way to incorporate affiliate marketing is for the blogger to review products and then link to the merchant selling the product at the end of the review. Any successful blog has a well-defined niche, and that is the attraction for merchants who wish to use affiliate marketing on blogs.

Another benefit of using blogs as affiliate marketing partners is that blogs can rank organically on search engines, therefore increasing their reach.

Social Media Influencers

Social media influencers are people who have developed a position of power and influence in a specific industry and exert and display that influence predominantly on social media and YouTube. Such influencers are common in the makeup, fashion, food, and music industries. Through their influence they can impact the purchase decisions of their followers. When influencers conduct affiliate marketing for merchants, there is more than one benefit for both parties. The affiliate marketer, in this case, will often receive free products to try out so that they can recommend it. The merchant, besides the sale, has the image of their product elevated as these influencers are often well-respected.

Microsites

A microsite is, as the name suggests, a smaller version of a bigger website. It often takes a larger product segment and divides it into a single, targeted call-to-action. An example of a microsite is Spotify's "Year in Music," which pops up once a year around December to allow users to see which artists they listened to most that year and get other stats related to their geographical market.

Email Lists

Email lists are linked to another platform, such as a website or blog, where users have subscribed to the email list or newsletter of that site. The emails sent out are then structured around the affiliate marketing link, and recipients are encouraged to follow the links to the merchant's page.

Large Media Websites

Considering the high traffic that large media and news websites get, they are ideal for affiliate marketing, especially with intermittent ads between content (Enfroy, 2019).

Using Social Media to Drive Your Affiliate Marketing Business

Social media is one of the most powerful marketing tools in an affiliate marketer's toolbox. It is used to generate traffic to your site, engage with your content, and increase the likelihood that you will have a click-through to your merchant's site.

To effectively use social media, you must understand how it works and where to find your target audience. There are many different social media platforms including Twitter, Facebook, Instagram, and Pinterest. Each of those platforms serve a different niche, purpose, and encourage users to engage in different ways. The key to knowing which platform to use is understanding your own audience demographic. It may seem best to represent yourself on all social media platforms, but this is actually counterproductive. You will never be able to put the same amount of effort into five different platforms, and it is necessary to choose one or two and work them well.

The following are essential strategies to employ when using social media to promote your affiliate marketing business.

Consistency

Most social media platforms work on algorithms that push consistent posters. To begin with, you will only be seen in your own followers' news feeds. If you continue to post consistently, however, and occasionally boost posts, your reach will start to increase. To be consistent, you can plan a week's-worth of social media posts, create them, and save them as drafts. Some social media platforms give you the facility to schedule future posts, and there are programs that can be used to manage your social media posting on your behalf.

Images and Video

Social media users are proven to prefer posts with images and videos. Instagram and YouTube are the two biggest video promotion platforms in the world. Posts with images and videos are shown to have a far higher engagement than text-only posts. When using images, ensure that they represent a positive idea.

Content Must Be Engaging

You are not using social media to push your affiliate links. You are using social media to direct traffic to the platform that holds your affiliate links. When social media users see blatant adverts in posts, they often consider it to be spam. The key is to create posts that are providing users with information or entertainment that encourages them to find more of the same on your platform. As with any group of users, you need to develop a relationship with your social media followers, let them see that you are adding value to their lives, and engage them in content that will direct traffic. Trust and reputation are imperative in social media (Germain, n.d.).

Chapter 4: Getting Started with Affiliate Marketing

In the previous chapter, we provided you with a deeper dive into affiliate marketing. Affiliate marketing is one of the easiest ways to get started earning passive income, but just like any other method, you are going to need to put in the work before you receive the reward. Once you have decided what type of platform you are going to use—blog, website, microsite, YouTube channel, podcast, influencer—you need to find merchants to be an affiliate for. The most important consideration is that the merchant fits your product niche, but this is not to say that if you blog about gardening you can only engage in affiliate marketing for merchants who have gardening products. Your audience, as well as having a specific interest, also has a demographic—age, gender, occupation, income, and location—which opens them up to other advertising that fits this demographic.

In looking for merchants to enter into affiliate marketing agreements, the greatest initial impact will come from affiliate networks.

What are Affiliate Networks

Affiliate networks are intermediaries that act as facilitators between affiliate marketers and merchants who wish to have their product or service promoted by affiliate marketers. They help each party to find the right fit for their platform or products. These networks are free to participate in, but they do generate their own revenue by taking either a share of the revenue earned by the affiliate marketer or charging a monthly subscription for the merchant to participate on their network.

An affiliate network will generally offer two ways for parties to generate revenue:

- Sharing revenue: the affiliate partner earns a share of the revenue generated by the sale that the merchant makes as a result of the affiliate partner's promotion.

- Fee for action: this is where the affiliate partner gets a set fee when a customer completes a specific action, e.g., PPC (Tipalti, n.d.).

Examples of Popular Affiliate Networks

Clickfunnels™ is a software program for online businesses to help increase their sales and market their products. Clickfunnels also has an affiliate network where you can promote the Clickfunnels products and generate income when one of the visitors to your platform use the services of Clickfunnels. The company offers a 40 % commission on the sales of Clickfunnels products or services, which is paid to the affiliate after a 45-day cooling-off period—to cover any refunds or returns. To become a Clickfunnels affiliate, you need to be a paying member of Clickfunnels (BigFoot Digital, n.d.).

Clickbank is the original affiliate network. It was established in 1998 and has 200 million customers across 190 countries. Clickbank is one of the easiest methods of affiliate marketing, which is why it is a good place for beginners to start. Its sign-up process is quick and easy, and you can use Clickbank as an affiliate marketer or a merchant. Clickbank has a large selection of products that you can be an affiliate for, and it pays high commissions. As with anything, though, there are some challenges with the network, including notoriously slow customer service. Another downside is that Clickbank charges you if your account is dormant and you make no sales within a specific period. If you want to start with Clickbank, be sure that you are representing products and brands with a good reputation and that you believe in. Keep in mind that by being an affiliate, you are linking your name to that product or service, and if things go wrong, your reputation could be impacted as well. Try the product and check online reviews. You should also do some research on the merchant in question to ensure that you are satisfied that they are a reputable brand (Nyathi, 2019).

JVZoo is another affiliate marketing network that leverages off the fact that its services are instantaneous. A benefit of JVZoo is that the tracking cookies last longer than 24-hours after your user has clicked the link. With JVZoo, your referral is automatically linked to any purchase that customer makes in the future too. So you don't just commission on one sale, you will receive a commission on anything they buy from that merchant in the future as well. JVZoo also pays instantly. As soon as the customer completes a purchase through your referral link, you will receive your commission. Should the customer request a refund at any time, you will be required to refund the commission paid to you. JVZoo only uses PayPal to pay affiliate marketers, so if you do not have access to PayPal you won't be able to use JVZoo. You need to apply to each JVZoo vendor separately, which could be time-consuming, depending on how many products you plan to be an affiliate for (Hofmann, n.d.).

How to Get Traffic to Your Platform

There are various methods of driving traffic to your platform, some of which we have already touched on:

- Paid advertising - this can include Google ads and ads on social media.

- Social media - we discussed this method in detail in Chapter 3.
- If you have a blog, try varying the length of your content to see what attracts more traffic.
- Write compelling headlines for your content.
- Optimize search engine optimization (SEO) techniques.
- Use popular keywords.
- Guest blogging - network with other blogs in your niche and write posts for them that will drive their readers to your site as well.
- Try LinkedIn - this platform is now much more than a job-hunting website (Shewan, 2019).
- YouTube channel - even if you are not monetizing through YouTube yet, you can use the platform to direct traffic to your site.
- If you have used the Kindle Direct Publishing service to publish a book, this is also an excellent way to drive traffic to your site.

How to Build a Landing Page that Converts

What is a Landing Page?

A landing page is a static page that is a part of your website or blog. It is usually the main entry-point for visitors to your platform, and it should provide them with a call-to-action to convert them to regular visitors to your page or to perform a specific action, such as reading a very specific piece of content or signing up to a newsletter. Getting the visitor to engage with your call-to-action is called 'conversion.' Conversion rates differ between niches, but the average conversion rate is about 3 %. Ideally, you want to be aiming for higher than average, which is around 11 %.

How to Encourage Conversion

There are various ways to encourage conversion, including the following:

- Use a single call-to-action. Make your intention for the visitor very clear, and only ask them to do one thing. You could be asking them to subscribe to a newsletter or click through to your latest content post. The instruction must be clear and easy to follow.

- The call-to-action must stand out on the landing page. Use contrasting colors and language that encourages action.
- Ensure that your call-to-action is in the line of sight as soon as a visitor arrives on your landing page. The should not have to scroll to find it.
- You will need to offer something in exchange for your visitor's conversion, and it needs to be valuable. A free document, book, course, or template can provide the value needed to secure their conversion.
- Include your unique value proposition. This is a statement that explains to your visitor how you plan to solve their problem or add value to their lives.
- Let people know how to get into contact with you. Social media information usually works well here.
- Include some great reviews or testimonials of your site.
- Your grammar and spelling must be absolutely flawless on your landing page. Any errors will cause your

visitor to wonder about the validity of your page.

- Don't overload the page. Too much information on your landing page is going to be confusing and drag your visitor's attention away from your call-to-action (Swain, 2018).

Low-Ticket vs. High-Ticket

An important consideration in setting up your affiliate marketing business is deciding whether you will be offering low-ticket or high-ticket products i.e., affordable or high-end.

Predominantly, this is going to depend on your niche. If you are marketing to parents of toddlers, they are likely already cash-strapped, so your best bet is marketing low-ticket items. If you are marketing to foodies who enjoy top-class food and restaurants, you can look at higher ticketed items. It is best to have a range and test out different prices to see what your audience is interested in. Even if your niche lends itself to higher ticketed items, it is always best to offer a lower cost alternative as well. Generally, people will only buy high-ticket items from businesses they know, so if you offer a lower cost version, you will be able to secure the customer for your merchant. Once that customer has used and enjoyed the product, they will likely come back for a higher ticketed item. You will usually sell more low-ticket items, so there is a possibility that you could generate more revenue by marketing low-ticket items than high-ticket items. High-ticket items, on the other hand, will give you a higher revenue in one go. The decision is always going to be based on your audience and their needs, so be sure to be intuitive about that when making the decision on the price range of products you will offer (Bullock, 2017).

Chapter 5: Strategizing for Your Selected Affiliate Business

In Chapter 4, we briefly discussed Clickfunnels and their affiliate network. In this chapter, we will delve deeper into this phenomenal software and discuss not only how it can help you make money from an affiliate perspective but also how it can be used to help you strategize for your online business as a whole.

Clickfunnels is a software package. It is not to be mistaken with a sales funnel, which is the sales jargon term for the process we place prospects in our business with the intention that they will be converted into new customers on the other end of that funnel. For non-digital businesses, a sales funnel will include events like meetings, presentations, and methods of closing the customer face-to-face. For online businesses, as we will only ever interact with our customers online, a sales funnel is the digital process we take our new visitors through to convert them into buying customers. Clickfunnels helps you to build sales funnels.

The biggest difference between any business' standard website and the development of a website with Clickfunnels is that if you go to a standard business website, you will find information on their products, who they are as a business, and where they operate. You will likely browse that website for a few minutes and then click out of it because there is no clear path for you to follow to any call-to-action. A website developed with Clickfunnels is built to guide you from the entry point through to the point of sale.

Clickfunnels does not build a website for you; it builds a sales funnel. If you go to the landing page of a site developed using Clickfunnels, you will not find the standard menus you would find on other websites such as 'about,' 'products,' 'services,' and "contact us." This is because a menu like this gives you too many options and with online businesses, options are the equivalent of distractions, and distractions lose sales.

When you access the landing page of a site built by Clickfunnels, you will find one available action—the call-to-action we discussed previously. Once you click on that call-to-action, the next step in the sales funnel will be a sales page where the customer can view information about the product that you are selling and enter their payment information. Clickfunnels helps you to add what is called an 'upsell' to the payment cart. An upsell is when your customer is already in buying mode, and you add something else to the package that increases the value to the customer and increases your revenue. An example could be a book that you are selling, and when your customer goes to purchase the book they receive an upsell request to also purchase your online course at a discounted rate. After your customer has committed to purchasing and entered their information, they will be taken to a full sales page that may include your high-ticket items. Clickfunnels saves the customer's purchase information (for that transaction only, not permanently) and if they click on any of your high-ticket items, it will automatically bill them. The reason for this is that, from a psychological perspective, if a customer has to enter their payment information a second time, they are far more likely to abandon the sale. The button that your customers click to buy high-ticket items has a disclaimer written on it that warns if they click that button they will be automatically billed.

Should the customer not wish to purchase the high-ticket item at that time, Clickfunnels inserts an option for them to decline the transaction, which takes them to a lower-cost alternative. The last step after all the sales pages is a thank you page that will either provide your customer with a free item you may have offered, or it provides links to follow you on social media. The idea behind Clickfunnels is to maximize your sales from your traffic but also to maximize the value you provide your customers (Buildapreneur, 2018).

Clickfunnels is the key to maximizing your marketing efforts. Not only is it a far easier way to build a sales site that is geared toward converting customers, once you are sold on it as a product and you can see its value in real terms, you can join their affiliate program and help others to improve their businesses while earning an affiliate commission.

Clickfunnels Affiliate Program

One you have used Clickfunnels in your online business, you are going to be sold on its value. When you are passionate about a product, it is much easier to sell.

Before we get into the specifics behind the Clickfunnels affiliate program, let us first cover a few terms that are used within the program which are important to understand:

- **Trial** - Clickfunnels offers a free 14-day trial. If you get someone to sign-up to a trial, Clickfunnels is not yet making any money and, therefore, neither do you. After the 14 days are up, however, they will need to either subscribe to Clickfunnels or forfeit the program. When they subscribe, you will earn money.
- **Monthly Recurring Revenue (MRR)** - Because Clickfunnels is a software program, the user is charged for the services they use on a monthly basis, which can be anywhere between $97 and $297 and the MRR comes in when you earn 40 % of that each month as an affiliate.

- **Churn** - This is not only an online business term but also a standard sales term. It means how many people naturally drop off from the program every month. This could happen for many reasons and may not have anything to do with something you or Clickfunnels has done. It is a very normal part of the sales process.
- **Painkiller or Vitamin** - You want to be marketing products that are painkillers and not vitamins. Vitamins are nice to have, but they are not necessary, whereas painkillers are necessary if you want to live a pain-free life. In other words, you want to be marketing a product that gives your customers a solution to their problem. Clickfunnels is a painkiller.

Once you are a paying member of Clickfunnels, you automatically qualify to be an affiliate. The following will guide to accessing your Clickfunnels affiliate account.

Inside the software, go to your profile picture, hold your mouse over it and you will see a tab labeled 'affiliate.' You will be taken to a page that will show you your earnings, and underneath it is all of the options of the various Clickfunnels products you can market.

Underneath the options, there is a button that reads, "Get My Affiliate Links." This takes you to the links that you will use to guide customers to the Clickfunnels website via your link and log their purchase as a sale for your affiliate account.

Once you have decided which of the Clickfunnels products you are going to market, you click on the "affiliate links" button, and it will take you to a page where you can copy your affiliate link. This link is embedded into your site.

Clickfunnels provides you with a host of marketing material to use in your campaign such as banner ads, instagram posts, and email ads.

Clickfunnels is the ultimate passive income generator because once you have signed someone up, you will earn that monthly recurring commission without doing anything else. Clickfunnels also has additional rewards for their affiliates besides their monthly commissions. Their current additional reward is that any affiliate who has more than 100 recurring subscribers on their account receives $500 per month toward their dream car. If you reach 200 recurring subscribers, you receive $1000 per month toward your dream car.

Clickfunnels also provides different products geared toward different audiences, for instance, if you happen to have a predominantly female audience, Clickfunnels has a product specifically designed for female E-preneurs. It is important to market Clickfunnels as a software program that solves the problems of online entrepreneurs. If you attempt to market Clickfunnels as a way to *start* a business, you are likely to have a far higher churn rate because that is a misrepresentation of what the product does. A good way to do this is by promoting Clickfunnels free 14-day trial. By doing this, you are promoting the software and nothing else.

Once you start signing customers up, the Clickfunnels affiliate page provides you with a wide range of statistics and numbers that you can use to manage your affiliate program.

The monthly recurring income generated from Clickfunnels is the key to your financial freedom. You don't just want one-of payments. Passive income needs to generate itself consistently, and that is exactly what Clickfunnels does (Crestani, 2019).

Conclusion

As the world changes, the economy changes with it. We can no longer rely solely on one company to provide us with the money we need to fund our lives and support our families. We have no choice but to start thinking outside the box. The world of passive income generation can be intimidating when you first look at it. How can it even be possible to earn money without actively working something every day?

Models of passive income have existed for many decades. Rental income and commission earned by financial consultants can both be considered forms of passive income. What we have done in this book is to convert that idea into online possibilities.

As with starting any business, you will need an entrepreneurial mindset, and let's be honest, not everyone is cut out to be an entrepreneur. Some people are far happier working for a boss at their 9 to 5 jobs, and there's really nothing wrong with if it makes you happy. It is risky to rely 100 percent on a

9 to 5 job with no back-up income. Circumstances can change in a second, and in the current economy, we have seen large businesses shut down overnight. If you think that you would be better off as a 9 to 5 worker, ask yourself, what would you do if you drove to work tomorrow morning and your employer had closed its doors? Everyone should have a back-up income whether you plan on being a permanent online entrepreneur or not.

We covered five of the most popular ways to generate passive income online. The method you choose is going to be based on your interests and skills as well as the audience you are trying to reach. Really, the smartest method is to try to include as many of these methods as possible, but we all have to start somewhere and affiliate marketing is the best place to start.

Traffic is key for online businesses. You want to draw traffic to your site, and you want to convert that traffic. We discussed the ways that social media can be used to drive traffic to your website. Remember, you cannot expect to be highly successful on every social media platform that exists. You must pick one or two that fits your audience and work those platforms hard. Once you've managed to generate traffic, you want to convert them through your landing page. We've provided you with some great tips on how to build a successful conversion landing page. Think about the last time you purchased something online. Now go to that business' landing page and analyze it. Ask yourself what made you want to interact with that page and how they drew you into the purchase. Now apply those elements to your own landing page.

We discussed the basics behind affiliate marketing—how to get started, what the different platforms are that can be used, and what affiliate networks are. We then took a deep dive into the quintessential passive income generation program—Clickfunnels. We discovered how we can use Clickfunnels to generate recurring monthly income all while adding value to our customers. The latter is a point you really want to focus on in your passive income generation journey. You don't want to just be selling 'stuff' for the sake of it. That will only serve to create a reputation for you that you are someone who only cares about making money, and you don't really care whether you are adding value or selling a reputable product. That may earn you a few sales, but in the long-term, it is going to damage your potential. Customers want to know that the person selling to them really cares about them and wants to sell them a product that is useful, valuable, and will solve their problems. That is also where relationship-building comes in. You cannot expect to open a website and start selling. You need to build relationships first.

In *How to Make Money on the Internet,* we have provided you with a way to circumvent the traditional, active income model. We have given you the keys to your financial, time, and location freedom. All you need to do now is take those keys and open the door.

References

23 tips for building a landing page that converts in 2018 - Agile CRM Blog. (2018, August 10). Retrieved December 10, 2019, from Agile CRM Blog website: https://www.agilecrm.com/blog/building-a-landing-page-that-converts/

25 Ways to Increase Traffic to Your Website. (2014). Retrieved December 10, 2019, from Wordstream.com website: https://www.wordstream.com/blog/ws/2014/08/14/increase-traffic-to-my-website

Anderson, V. (2018, June 20). An Inside Look at the Mindset of a Successful Entrepreneur. Retrieved December 10, 2019, from Oberlo website: https://www.oberlo.com/blog/mindset-successful-entrepreneur

Ayodeji Awosika. (2019, March 21). Kindle Direct Publishing: How to Make Real Money on Amazon. Retrieved December 10, 2019, from Smart Blogger website: https://smartblogger.com/kindle-publishing/#common_questions

E-preneur: The Growth of Online Entrepreneurship Infographic. (2015).

Retrieved December 10, 2019, from
Lucrazon.com website:
http://www.lucrazon.com/growth-of-
online-entrepreneurship

Gennifer Carragher. (2018, December 12).
Amazon FBA in 2019: How It Works
(Benefits + Disadvantages). Retrieved
December 10, 2019, from The BigCommerce
Blog website:
https://www.bigcommerce.com/blog/amaz
on-fba/#14-tactics-to-successfully-sell-on-
amazon-fba

How Does Clickfunnels Affiliate Program
Work? [YouTube Video]. (2019). Retrieved
from
https://www.youtube.com/watch?v=NBCo
Zb6g0ok

How to Make Money on YouTube: 6
Effective Strategies. (2019, August 8).
Retrieved December 10, 2019, from
Hootsuite Social Media Management
website: https://blog.hootsuite.com/how-
to-make-money-on-youtube/

How To Make Money With Clickfunnels:
Becoming A Clickfunnels Affiliate. (2016).
Retrieved December 10, 2019, from SEO

Company in Barnsley | Social Media Marketing Agency in Yorkshire website: https://www.bigfootdigital.co.uk/clickfunn els-affiliate-program

https://www.facebook.com/adamenfroydot com. (2018, July 27). Affiliate Marketing in 2019: What It Is + How Beginners Can Start. Retrieved December 10, 2019, from The BigCommerce Blog website: https://www.bigcommerce.com/blog/affilia te-marketing/#how-does-affiliate-marketing-work

https://www.facebook.com/meetana. (2012, September 4). Ana Hoffman. Retrieved December 10, 2019, from TrafficGenerationCafe.com website: https://trafficgenerationcafe.com/jvzoo-affiliate-marketing/

Lilach Bullock. (2017, May 19). High ticket vs low ticket – which is more valuable to your business? Retrieved from LilachBullock website: https://www.lilachbullock.com/high-ticket-sales-low-ticket/

Pj Germain. (2019, June 18). How to Use Social Media to Drive Your Affiliate

Marketing. Retrieved December 10, 2019, from Pure Residuals website: https://pureresiduals.com/how-to-use-social-media-to-drive-your-affiliate-marketing/

Qhubekani Nyathi. (2019, July 24). ClickBank: The Brutally Honest, Must-Read Guide for 2020. Retrieved December 10, 2019, from Smart Blogger website: https://smartblogger.com/clickbank/

What EXACTLY Is ClickFunnels - An Inside Look [YouTube Video]. (2018). Retrieved from https://www.youtube.com/watch?v=9T92osOWYkE

What is an affiliate network? (2015). Retrieved December 10, 2019, from Tipalti website: https://tipalti.com/customers/affiliate-networks-tipalti/what-is-an-affiliate-network/

What Is Dropshipping | How Does Drop Shipping Work? (2016). Retrieved December 10, 2019, from Shopify website: https://www.shopify.co.za/guides/dropshipping/understanding-dropshipping

Adams, R. (2019). 17 Passive income ideas for increasing your cash flow. Retrieved from https://www.entrepreneur.com/slideshow/299914

Ferriss, T. (2009). *The 4-hour workweek: Escape 9-5, live anywhere, and join the new rich*. New York, New York: Crown Publishers.

Fiebert, A. (2019). 31 Passive income ideas to get you off the hamster wheel. Retrieved from https://www.listenmoneymatters.com/passive-income-ideas/

Gabrielle, Gundi. *Passive income freedom: 23 Passive income blueprints to go step-by-step from complete beginner to $5,000-10,000/month in the next 6 months*. 2019. Retrieved from https://www.amazon.com/Passive-Income-Freedom-Step-Step-ebook/dp/B07MDTMDCR

Guillebeau, C. (2017). *Side hustle: From idea to income in 27 days*. New York, New York: Crown Business.

Hogan, C. (2019). What is passive income and how do I build it? Retrieved from https://www.daveramsey.com/blog/what-is-passive-income

James Royal. (2019). 10 passive income ideas to help you make money in 2019. Retrieved from https://www.bankrate.com/investing/passive-income-ideas/

Mason, A. (2019). 30 Passive income ideas you can use to build real wealth. Retrieved from https://thecollegeinvestor.com/16399/20-passive-income-ideas/

Percy, R. (2019). *Passive income ideas for 2020: A step by step guide to easy passive income ideas for 2020 and beyond.* New York, New York: Amazon Digital Services LLC - Kdp Print Us.

Rose, J. (2019). Passive income ideas: 10 strategies to earn $1,000 per month. Retrieved from https://www.forbes.com/sites/jrose/2019/02/07/passive-income-ideas-2019/#2e650e0f14d3

FREE VIDEO

LEARN HOW TO MAKE $10,000 /MONTH FROM HOME

- Completely free (value of $197)
- Step by Step video course
- The fastest and easiest way to make a passive income in 2020
- Instant access
- Free Mastermind Support Group included

*Visit **www.sixfigures.info** to learn more*

www.ingramcontent.com/pod-product-compliance
Lightning Source LLC
Chambersburg PA
CBHW071658210326
41597CB00017B/2241